Crazy Quilt
of
Loss & Love

Diane Rudov

WORD ASSOCIATION PUBLISHERS
www.wordassociation.com
1.800.827.7903

Designed and published by
Word Association Publishers
205 Fifth Avenue
Tarentum, Pennsylvania 15084

www.wordassociation.com
1.800.827.7903

Library of Congress Cataloging-in-Publication Data

Names: Rudov, Diane, Author.
Title: Crazy Quilt of Loss and Love / Diane Rudov
Description: First Edition. | Poetry
Identifiers: ISBN 9781633853850
Subjects: Poetry

DAUGHTERS

Appears on page 95
2011 Signatures
Prose and Poems and Photos
Osher Lifelong Learning Institute at CMU, Volume 1V,
Spring 2011

This poem also won third prize in Adult Poetry Contest at
Chautauqua Institute in 1999

AUTUMN MEMORIES

Appears on page 161
Covenant of the Generation New Prayers, Poems, and
Meditations
Publisher WRJ, 2013

Additionally published in
Remembrance and Spirituality
Volume 3, June 2012, Temple Sinai Neshama
Center for Jewish Spirituality
Kol Ha-Neshama
Voice of the Spirit

Preface

Crazy Quilt of Loss and Love was written over the past thirty years through an autobiographical lens. This poetry collection captures the universal experiences of loss, redesigning a satisfying life, and adapting to the tumults of aging, illness, and death.

A "crazy quilt" is a collage comprised of varied shapes of mismatched fabrics. Originally, the poor created blankets from worn clothing and seed sacks to warm their families. Later, affluent Victorians designed quilts from silk fabrics, lavishly embroidering them. Despite their differing goals, these quilters shared the same process.

I view life itself as a "crazy quilt," complete with the zigzags of joy and sorrow. In each of this book's five sections, I weave together words, rather than fabrics, to tell a complete story. Like those who used scraps to make coverlets and the women who embellished taffetas, I have taken vestiges of my life and my observations about aging and death, transforming them into a "crazy quilt" of poems.

-Diane Rudov

CRAZY QUILT

You are my crazy quilt
stitched during winter storms,
comforting me as I merge
your triangles into squares.

I mend the remnants of my life,
splice your fresh beauty from old fabrics.
Once broken, I triumph by suturing
my heart with quilting threads.

CONTENTS

Unraveling

Somber poems describe the fraying of a marriage as it
moves towards divorce. The quilter begins to decide
what parts of clothing or fabric might be discarded
from its current life and what should be salvaged to
create something beautiful and useful.

SURVIVAL

I remember feeling like a fisherman's wife,
waiting for my lost husband,
keening and keeling when his letter arrived.

He was staying at a port; but his ship had not sunk.
I wailed from inside my suburban widow's walk,
wishing a squall had snatched him.

No funeral wake for him,
yet I buried a marriage of thirty years,
knowing I lacked ample time to trust again.

I remember, like a graying Ophelia,
braiding a garland for my short curly hair,
hoping a wind would whirl me away.

No funeral wake for me.
Slowly, I recalled the prickly days,
vowing to sway to my own breezes.

ATTRACTION

You extend your hand; I leap onto a high tightrope,
tossing safety aside to take risky steps with you.

When the wire frays, I yearn to fall gracefully.
Forfeiting the thrills, I crash to earth, damaged.

Friends weave safety nets, anchor and swaddle me.
They spoon-feed love medicine tinged with hope.

Now I like stepping firmly on solid ground.
I don't envy birds in flight, the hand-glider's surge.

Even so, I know that someday when I am dying
I may crave to hold your hand until I let go.

LAMENT

Tell me you loved me.
Tell me I didn't squander half my life.
Tell me we created our babies through love.

Tell me I didn't toss away thirty years
like a cluster of bold balloons released to the sky.

Tell me you know our son has my smile and your eyes.
Tell me you miss me and our bursts of joy.

Then maybe I'll know again when
my heartsounds are true and clear.

DUELING

You forge my trust into a golden shield,
blinding me with guarantees
that I am your world.

You thrust and parry,
protected by my blind faith,
lulling me with smiles and words.

Now I know that truth melts metal.

MASQUERADES

I want to study your familiar face,
pinch it to know what is true.
Your mysteries weary me.

No poker face I, my emotions obvious,
you read and adjust your façade to mine.
Aware at last, I disconnect from you,
expecting my spirit to be free.

But my face now reveals the
grim mask of Greek tragedy.
Sunless sorrow blights my
hopes for tomorrow.

MIXED MESSAGES

Friends and family support me.
Through their calls, they remind me
I exist to them,
if not always to myself.
They voice my childhood name,
recall our shared histories.

The same friends and family distress me,
praise my strength,
hoping I can expunge you and tainted times.
They try to protect me,
ignoring our contented days.

Why do friends and family pretend the same
memories bonding me to them
don't tie me to you?
One swipe across a chalkboard cannot
erase thirty years of a marriage.

Throwing away old black and white photographs
does not destroy
their stories, even if I burned
the negatives.

Assembling

Poems focus on positive family memories and provide relief from prior stark grief. These represent the special parts that have been saved by the quilter for an eventual coverlet.

PRESTO PASSAGES

Within this silence
my thoughts migrate to former years,
crave to hug the four blond jewels there,
dancing, glistening in the fold.

I wish to slow the moon and sun,
to hold close my universe.
But time and love weave links of leaving.
I blink and my children
shimmer away.

JOURNEYS

This trip, a joyful baptism of travel
with my adult daughter, immerses me in sad memories.

I gasp for air, struggling to enjoy the celebration
while the past threatens to pull me under.

She steers me down Florence's narrow walkways,
winces as I fearfully drift when I'm on my own,
prods me to gain a clearer sense of direction.

I yearn to mirror her independence
and grieve that I deferred growing my own.

I commit to placing a compass
close to my heart to guide me.

Each day the rites of travel ease our tensions.
Embracing, we witness a Venetian sunset.

The moon shadows the murky canals, ironically
purifying old wounds.

NATIVE SONS

I imagine my condo as the homestead farm,
my sons residing on two parcels of land,
near enough if I send an alarm.

They never craved to be pioneers.
Instead, each developed his world where rooted,
knowing they can travel to other spheres.

They have discovered an art to being content in place,
meshing the familiar with the unknown,
knowing they are surrounded by grace.

DAUGHTERS

I am not a frontierswoman.
I linger east, bonded to crisp crimson leaves,
daffodils that stare down the snow.

More venturesome, perhaps, my daughters
settle in foggy, moist cities where other
eastern daughters declare their own territory.

Sunday calls connect us now.
We talk of kittens, quilting, and careers.
Like fireflies, we light in and out of each other's lives
until the next work week wanes.

I question my solitude and crave
the quilting-bee chatter of pioneer women.
Their ghosts gossip about our
sharing coffee and cake once a year.

Do the kisses and calico snippets I mail
last all the way to those foggy, moist cities?

Is there a quilting hoop round enough
to connect us across the miles?

FAMILY DUET

My grandbaby and I play in harmony.
She sways in her wound-up musical swing,
floats forward, babbles, drifts back.
I perch nearby at my upright piano,
stumbling through a Haydn sonata.

The maestro conducts,
thumbs tracing in the air,
jiggling her turkey-thigh legs.
Her swing tick-tick-ticks
the metronome beat
as I jerkily roam the keyboard.

I pray her steady glide
hints a life without drama.
When coasting stops,
she mourns music gone.
I hold her and croon
of twinkling stars.

She coos and smiles at my song.
Together, we waft through
space, sound, time.

UNREMARKABLE I

My mother and I share Sunday morning coffee.
She sips her black brew while I, miles away,
grind beans.
I feed my cat as we mosey into our chatting spree.
We pick up the pace, probe a <u>New Yorker</u> piece.
She marvels at a crossword puzzle clue.
I critique a movie and my new lease.

This Sunday a silent phone chills me with fear.
My mother drinks coffee in a hospital room
while I, miles away, brace for news I must bear.
We await news of an MRI, life's crystal ball.
Will its predictions cast a black pall?
What will we talk about in our future calls?

I tell friends my mother cannot die or be lame.
"Yes, she can," say these veterans of this pain.
I rebut that there can be no wild tumor.
A lifetime later, she calls and proclaims that
the test shows hers is not lethal.

UNREMARKABLE II

My daughter and I share Sunday morning coffee.
I sip my brew while she, miles away, grinds beans.
Sitting in our kitchens, we mosey into a chatting spree.
I describe a <u>New Yorker</u> piece, a new blouse.
She critiques an indie movie and her latest gig.

This silent Sunday I rest in a hospital
while my daughter waits near her phone,
trying to banish fears of my doom.
We await MRI results, today's crystal ball.
Will they steal joy from our future calls?

She says she's told friends I cannot die or be lame.
"Not true," say they, veterans of this pain.
At last my doctor ends this "What If?" game,
stating I have a truly unremarkable brain.

Redesigning

Poems depict the struggle to create a new life from a former one. The quilter focuses on creating beauty from what is at hand after the winnowing. This is the time to imagine a new whole, deciding how to merge fabrics, colors, shapes.

TRUMPETS IN A MINOR MODE

I raise my baton to signal.
Let the trumpets proclaim
my journey to a new life.

When the music begins, I am free.
I exorcise my role of wife,
like a snake shedding its skin.

I clear the sky of clouds
and shoot for joy,
splurge on theater tickets, tour Italy.

Even before the trumpet chords wane,
I ponder if I can sustain my odyssey,
struggling to not douse my high spirits.

I realize I have sold myself snake oil
when I start to believe my comforting kittens
can meet my needs for touch.

I raise the baton again.
Let the trumpets proclaim
my journey to a new life…

PECKING ORDER

Happy holidays

Honeymoon holidays

Harmonious holidays

High Holidays

Holy holidays

Hallowed holidays

Hollowed holidays

Hurt holidays

Hot holidays

Hole-in-my-heart holidays

Hellish holidays

Haul-me-away holidays

FREE WILL

The initial race to freedom slows.
I stumble in my marathon,
searching for the new me,
quicksanded.

Years ago I moved to a Main-Street town,
as a bride flailing at its smallness.
Through time I glued myself to my mate,
securing the fastening.

Now I can reside wherever I wish.
I vacillate among possible moves,
awed by the array of choices.
An amateur at playing alone, I hesitate.

How I envy long-distance runners
who are decisive
and never flinch
from their goal.

MODERN MATCHMAKING

The middle-aged stranger, seeking a mail order bride,
distills himself into an online dating profile,
records his phone greeting in a resonant voice.

Wishing I knew the village matchmaker,
I study her cold proxy, a laptop website,
and convince myself the man summons me.

We audition each other over coffee.
I ask myself if he has sent a stand-in.
His tight bitter words don't match our calls.

I push aside an imaginary veil to find the real man,
as at a class reunion we search a face
to locate its smoother version.
But I cannot detect his essence.

I dismiss his concocted self.
How I yearn for Yenta, my babushked broker,
to find me a true connection.

THE GRADUATE

I dream I parade across a stage
in a black cap and gown to receive
a degree for beginning my new life.
When I awaken, I realize
I must retake the class.

Memories lurk about and
mock my hope to graduate from grief.
I still miss dancing with my ex-husband,
set a plate for him at a dinner party.

To convince myself the marriage
is dead I bury the past,
dig deeply and inter a coffee can
crammed with wedding photos,
then plant a rose bush atop the grave.

After entombing my lost dreams,
I mulch with confetti from shredded
love letters.

RELAPSE

Happiness and I are close friends now.
Before then, loss ambushed my soul,
numbing all pleasure pulses,
sabotaging my efforts to outwit it.

Loss refused to surrender until
evicted by parched tears,
slithering away to invade
another broken heart.

Why the melancholy today?
I'm jumpy, fearing arrival of a gloomy message.
But my logic sentry informs all is well,
no grief appears at the gate this autumn day.

I wonder if my raking leaves scratches
open old wounds
or if I dread
warming my own chilled toes.

Joy can vanish in a flash.
I question if happiness is loyal enough to me
to risk playing duets with my neighbor
or simmering a pot of lentil soup for two.

MOVING ON

Father of my children, I toast you.
May the fruits of our entwinings bring you joy.

May you pray with them over the Sabbath wine,
cheer together for your favorite teams.
May new memories match earlier ones.

Let us toast to our positive past and
to their dreams as the champagne flows
at their weddings and births
of our grandchildren.

Transforming

These poems celebrate a newly-found, satisfying life. The quilter recognizes what feels right and true through time and stitches together these pieces. The result is their metamorphosis into a satisfying comforter.

PAUSE

Couples rashly rush
towards a marital crash.
The two of us, cautious souls,
meet and hesitate.

We linger to fathom depths,
question worries of buoyancy.

Our embers of infatuation
slowly kindle kisses and caresses,
stoking sparks until our hearts
can pledge a true love connection.

HOUSE-CHILLING

Listen!

You have been my home for thirty years and now new
owners knock.
They must delay their house-warming.
I am house-chilling, and you are not cooperating.
I thought we had an understanding.
I painted and pampered you; you warmly welcomed me
home. Now you merely flaunt your beauty.
Why don't you accept that I must leave you?

Working hard to detach from you,
I rub your Vermont slate tiles to absorb them into my
palms;
scrub off fingerprints, remembering the children who
created them.
I remove paintings and photos, trying to make your walls
anonymous.

I wave incense to whisk out bad spirits.
I thank you for your shelter,
for your willingness to adapt from the zany wallpaper
patterns of my youth to the calmer ones of maturity.

I plan to hand my key to the new owners tomorrow.
If the pear tree blossoms overnight,
I may have to delay til the next day.
Then I will tell them our secrets: where the hyacinths
sleep; which cubbyholes are best for hide and seek.

Meanwhile, don't try to hinder me
while I transform you, my home, back into a house.
I shall dance around in your empty spaces
one last time before we end our romance.

TO MY BRIDEGROOM

You are my balladeer,
serenading me with your violin and voice,
transforming my golden days into Technicolor,
stunning me with our similarities.

My knight in tweed jacket, you
impress me with your maturity and wit.

My soul mate, you
know with a glance when we are in sync.

Come close.
Press your heart to mine.
Marvel at how the rhythms
make you and me a we.

AWAKENINGS

I greet the dawn, satisfied you are near,
luxuriating in this ordinary day,
waiting to share laughter, a special kiss,
joy from a Mozart quartet.

We savor sweet choices.
Shall we relax together
or be with family and friends
or embark on an adventure?

When evening comes,
I know you will hold me,
whisper words of contentment,
seed deeper feelings of love.

I greet the dawn.
Each day I thrive, feeling treasured.

LONELINESS

People parade through my days and nights
at meetings and dinners
linked by long ribbons of words
and lattices of social bonds.
These total a sum of nothingness
unless, when I return home,
I can talk about it all
with a you
that makes
me a we.

REALITY CHECK

Only an Alpine skier would choose to hike Lothrop,
a steep Pittsburgh route I must ascend today.
I aim my slanted body towards its peak.

Thighs throb, hamstrings balk.
I fear losing momentum if I stop to rest.
The slope surprises my heart,
pulsing quickly as I tow myself upward.

Reaching my destination, I rest until
my lungs recover from the insult,
enabling calm, smooth thumps.

My body adapts sooner than my spirit,
believing youthful gumption
can outwit age.

THE GAMBLER

Gardening with abandon,
I imperil unclad arms, shunning all lotion,
exposing mottled legs to cancerous rays.

Fling brimmed bonnet into the shade,
gift cranky knees with a low stool perch,
dirty, naked hands toss the earth.

There's heavy action in my Eden today,
sowing perennials for future seasons,
planting with joy and real abandon.

I lay odds on their blooming each year,
staking my memory on a risky notion,
still unprotected from harm.

THE DRIVER

I steer through the sun glare,
driving old friends to a doctor.
He, sick and in pain, lies on the back seat.
She, his wife, sits primly in the front.

We share no words.
Autumn pantomimes their story
through its doomed beauty,
a prelude of the harshness to come.

Hours later, the terrible verdict arrives.
Silently, in the rear-view mirror,
I steal glances to gauge
the mood of their erratic love.

She cradles his head in her lap,
gazing at him in a way
most would envy.

Patching

Humans, like quilts, frequently need mending, proof of the cliché, "After 70, it is patch, patch, patch." The poems in this largest section focus on losses, such as disability, illness, and death of loved ones. We, like a quilt, need strong bindings to hold us together during these struggles.

DAZE

My friend transfers eggs,
one by one, into the fridge door,
then drifts and returns them
to their cardboard nests.

It is only three months since the
stroke jinxed her thinking,
dimming her mind's pilot light.

She sleepwalks through each day.
If she dozes, it takes time
when she awakes to grasp
where she is in space.

She cracks one of the eggs,
freeing a perfect yolk,
a tiny, steadying feat transforming
the egg into something other
than it once was, too.

SING-ALONG

A stroke strangles her words.
I wonder how much she grasps mine.
We study each other.
Her placid face does not share.

She remains mute as others sing.
When the guitarist strums,
"I'll Be Loving You Always,"
melody liberates memory.

She gazes adoringly at me,
demonstrating perfect pitch and timing,
repeating and repeating
"Always."

I am relieved she does not know
that I am a stranger.

TALL TALES

He tells me I am still beautiful.
I believe I never was.
I tell him he remains handsome.
In fact, he still is.

He says he feels healthy.
I know it isn't true.
He worries I am unwell.
I say I am fine.

We tease and share
our myths, mostly harmless lies.
We are actually fraught
with fears of disappearing.

BENEDICTION

Father of my children,
I hope our sons and daughters
can comfort you through
your illness.

I watch sadly as their tears
cascade happy memories
that cannot dilute
their feelings of loss.

Their grief pulls me back to
your bedside, where we
ease each other
into an honest peace.

DEADLINE

The closer my friend creeps to ninety
the more urgently she speaks,
blurting out curt words that hurt.

As a tot she spoke what she thought
until her folks taught her grace and tact
and she subscribed to compassion.

No time for niceties today.
She zings, attacks, dismays,
knowing she has much more to say.

DISGUISES

I wouldn't have noticed if he'd said, "Hi, honey,"
But my friend utters, "Hello, darling."
I welcome him to an exercise class where
we senior gymnasts know he has dementia.
Still handsome, his authentic self is in absentia.

We grasp hands as I view him with fondness.
A good soul, he tries to hide his amnesia
by calling me this term of endearment.
I do not hear it as intimate, but startling,
from a man who now knows many darlings.

Later I brood that I cannot summon a friend's name.
Igniting my long-term memory, it merely flickers.
Perhaps a person of my age gets a grace period
to recall a chum.

I wonder if I'll be as kind, if my mind ever limps to lame,
as my gallant friend who pretends he knows.

KINDRED CARING

How strange that we fled the safe place that helped him to
survive.
We are the bride and groom of elopement joy, giddy at
being home.
I replace the gloved hands of nurses with my soothing
strokes, supplant IV tubes that fed him life with my barley
soup.

Today I wash my husband on his new shower bench,
scrubbing his shoulders, strong from lifting weights for
years, dabbing a soapy washcloth over his weakened,
scarred legs. The warm water subdues his pain.

I cheer as he takes tentative toddler steps with his walker,
protecting him by moving like I'm a larger person in a
smaller space.
No violins crescendo, no images blur with our slow-
motion scene.
My life itself narrows for now; a road once-wide has
become a footpath.

Each time we sanctify his body, he gains a stronger will to
live, allowing me to view the final Jewish ritual
as a desert mirage.
Neither of us is ready for his body to be cleansed and
purified by strangers who softly murmur prayers for the
dead.

WHEN I BECOME MY MOTHER

Each New Year's Eve my mother attended
the Vienna Philharmonic concert in her nightgown.
Her robed sister, far away, also savored Strauss music.

Both widows gloomed from solitude.
Later they would lift their own quarantines,
critique the violins with keen ears,
clink champagne glasses against their phones.

Now each New Year's my husband and I
enjoy that same Austrian orchestra.
He can no longer waltz or slow dance,
but we sit close, swaying to the violins.

We clang glasses of apple juice,
toasting to each other's health,
wondering about the music of next year.

METAMORPHOSIS

I am an illness virgin,
pumping iron in aerobics class,
strutting as I carry grocery bags,
Tarzan's Jane, strong and cocky.

I wonder, as I steer towards eighty,
why I am so blessed.
When my luck runs out someday,
will I feel any less anointed?

Suddenly, I lose my maidenhood.
My marred heart beats steadily
while struggling to pump out its glitches.
I reel from the blow.

I preview my funeral,
guessing now who might attend.
Friends pay homage with hugs and soups,
speaking words unsaid before.

I had been innocent of illness.
Now I learn to treat my body more gently,
to accept this new me as no less,
still intact, despite being transformed.

CLARITY

Dormant, I rest in bed to heal,
tamping down embers of shoulds.
I feel anonymous
to myself.

You arrive with golden soup,
nectar of the gods.
Foggy, I wiggle sideways to upright myself,
hoping my essence will surface through the haze.

I focus on wobbly steps to reach you,
calming when you show your delight.
We loop arms while you shepherd me
through the lessening blur.

With you, I recognize who I am.

TAKING TURNS

No worrying about what to wear today.
We eighty-year-olds know the drill.
A friend's death summons our uniforms,
black outfits we wore too often this year.

No pattern exists in how we mourn each loss.
No calming psalms ease the pain,
while we shrinking survivors soldier on.

A few eulogies spark memories of levity,
relaxing us enough to recall childhood fun
when we used to circle, circle, prepare for the
music to halt—watch!
We are down one chair.

Now we busily amuse ourselves,
sweetening bonus hours,
hoping luck and grit
might score more years.

We wonder when we will be tagged It
or "You're out!" as we drift to home base.

WIDOWHOOD

A tsunami scoops me away from safety,
drags me into the sea where
I flounder, trying to keep afloat.
When I wearily return to shore,
my world is transformed.

I rush to see you, my spouse,
but you, dear friend, are nowhere.
Why did you leave me so soon?
Later, I wait for you to come to bed.
Why aren't you whispering to me?

I avoid silence, which begets sadness,
weep when I hear our music by myself.
I grieve our special oneness
and my former steady self.

I think of you now as a dying patient.
When will I remember the vibrant you?
I yearn to recall our waltzing days.
Meanwhile, I sob salty ocean tears,
reminding me of when I last saw you.

THE RECLINER

I always found my husband in his
oversized leather recliner.
He would sink into it from his wheelchair,
sighing in this refuge
where he felt the least pain.

He relished being a star athlete.
A victory now meant transferring
without falling from his transport.
His world had shrunk but he was still within it.
Phones and remotes kept him connected,
surrounding him with love, news, and music.

He is gone.
The scarred chair remains in place,
not a sign of my denial of his death
but of respect to a cherished family member.

The recliner cradled him in a way I could not do.
It is my perpetual Cup of Elijah,
wistfully saving a seat,
but knowing he will never return.

A CONVERSATION

Our Christmas cactus bloomed today,
shooing away the winter gloom.
The sole pink flower promises
its siblings soon will present themselves.

If you were here, you would ask how the plant
knows today is actually Christmas;
I would answer I don't know.
You would ponder if it blooms in January
for Russian Orthodox believers;
I would respond, I hope so.

You would wonder about its Latin name and grab a
dictionary,
announcing we have a "Schlumbergera."
I would say, you're a thorough researcher.
Thanks for watering it each Sunday.

You would report it grew first in Brazil;
I would say I plan to snip the flower for our kitchen table.
You would speculate if it adheres to the lunar or solar
calendar;
I would say I don't care.

Our syncopated chatter exists only in my memory.
I am here and you are "there," wherever "there" is.

QUIRKS OF TIME

I once tried to coax more time from the clock,
seeking to slow minutes on my watch.

Now I invest no effort
in stretching time.
I trudge through the minutes
except when with those I love.

Big Ben chimes more faintly each year.
June so quickly becomes July,
another healthy friend is gone.

Time seems low on elasticity,
never expanding, nothing
like my loving heart.

WA